EASTER COLORII
FOR ADULTS AND TEENS

MW01242265

This coloring book belongs to:

_____

_____

Hannah Siegert

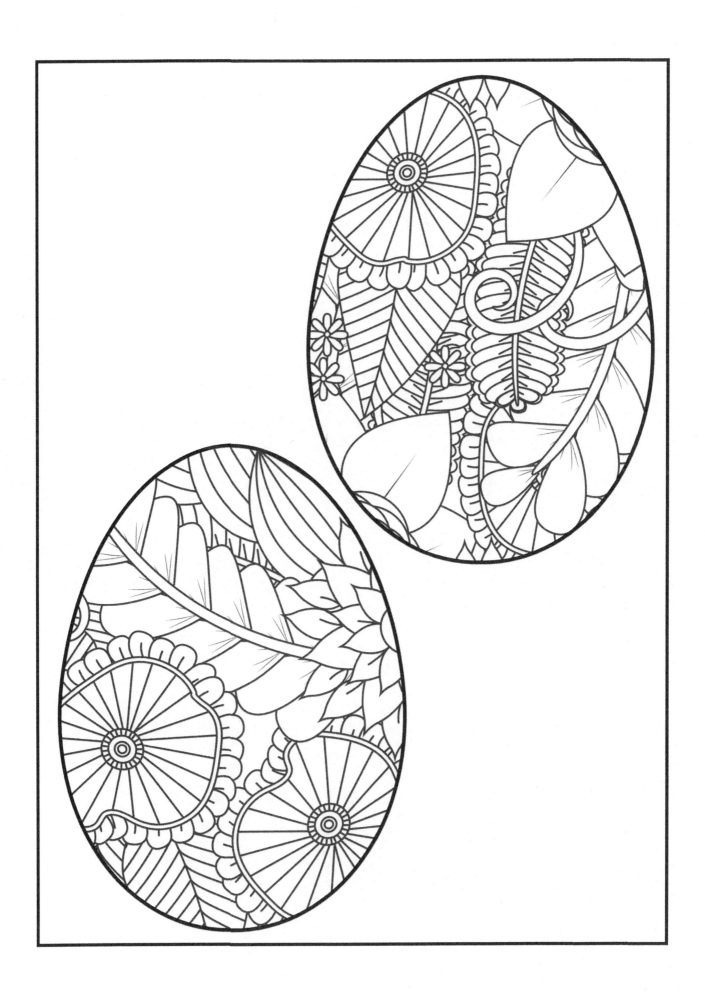

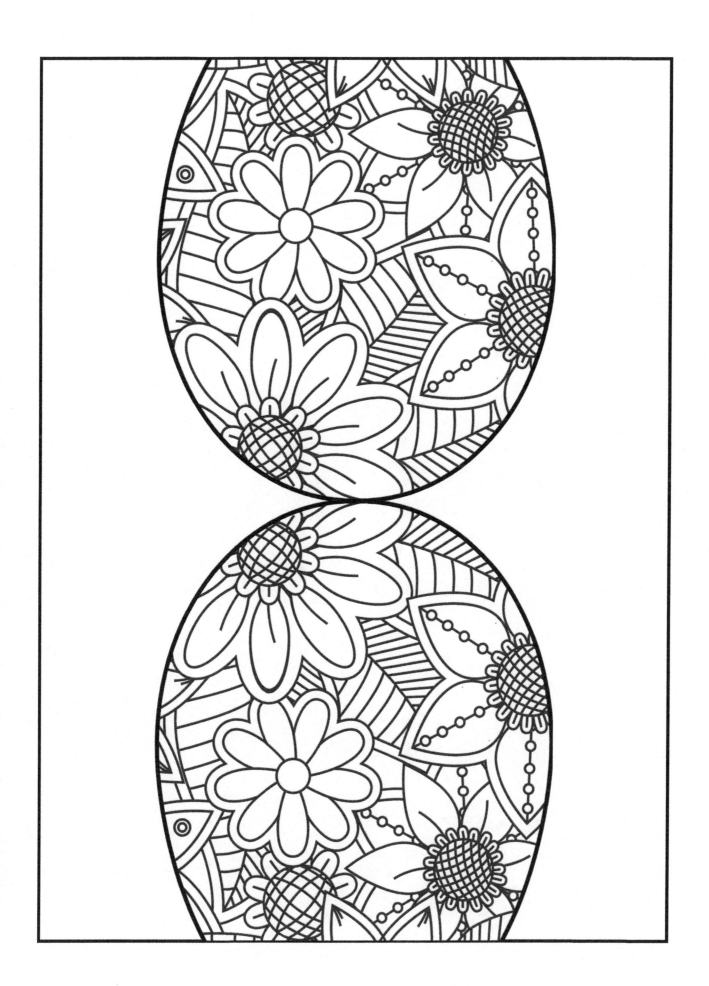

♥ **Thank you for your purchase** ♥

We hope that you enjoyed our coloring book.
Customer satisfaction is very important to us!

If you like this coloring book or have any
Questions? Concerns? Comments?
please send us your feedback at:

siegertpublishing@gmail.com

Your opinion matters :)

© Copyright 2023 - All rights reserved.

You may not reproduce, duplicate or send the contents of this book without direct written permission from the author. You cannot hereby despite any circumstance blame the publisher or hold him or her to legal responsibility for any reparation, compensation, or monetary forfeiture owing to the information included herein, either in a direct or an indirect way.

Made in the USA
Middletown, DE
27 March 2023

27760255R00060